VOLLEYBALL

Approaching the Net

PREPARING FOR GAME DAY

BASEBALL & SOFTBALL: SUCCESS ON THE DIAMOND

BASKETBALL: STRATEGY ON THE HARDWOOD

CHEERLEADING: TECHNIQUES FOR PERFORMING

EXTREME SPORTS: POINTERS FOR PUSHING THE LIMITS

FOOTBALL: TOUGHNESS ON THE GRIDIRON

LACROSSE: FACING OFF ON THE FIELD

SOCCER: BREAKING AWAY ON THE PITCH

TRACK & FIELD: CONDITIONING FOR GREATNESS

VOLLEYBALL: APPROACHING THE NET

WRESTLING: CONTENDING ON THE MAT

PREPARING FOR GAME DAY

VOLLEYBALL
Approaching the Net

Peter Douglas

MASON CREST

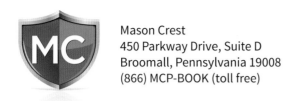

Mason Crest
450 Parkway Drive, Suite D
Broomall, Pennsylvania 19008
(866) MCP-BOOK (toll free)

First printing
9 8 7 6 5 4 3 2 1

ISBN (hardback) 978-1-4222-3921-6
ISBN (series) 978-1-4222-3912-4
ISBN (ebook) 978-1-4222-7876-5

Cataloging-in-Publication Data on file with the Library of Congress

QR CODES AND LINKS TO THIRD-PARTY CONTENT

CONTENTS

KEY ICONS TO LOOK FOR:

Words to understand: These words with their easy-to-understand definitions will increase the reader's understanding of the text while building vocabulary skills.

Sidebars: This boxed material within the main text allows readers to build knowledge, gain insights, explore possibilities, and broaden their perspectives by weaving together additional information to provide realistic and holistic perspectives.

Educational Videos: Readers can view videos by scanning our QR codes, providing them with additional educational content to supplement the text. Examples include news coverage, moments in history, speeches, iconic sports moments and much more!

Text-dependent questions: These questions send the reader back to the text for more careful attention to the evidence presented there.

Research projects: Readers are pointed toward areas of further inquiry connected to each chapter. Suggestions are provided for projects that encourage deeper research and analysis.

Series glossary of key terms: This back-of-the book glossary contains terminology used throughout this series. Words found here increase the reader's ability to read and comprehend higher-level books and articles in this field.

 ## WORDS TO UNDERSTAND:

electrolyte: any of the ions (e.g., sodium or calcium) that in biological fluid regulate or affect most metabolic processes (i.e., flow of nutrients into and waste products out of cells)

jeopardy: exposure to or imminence of danger

restorative: having the ability to make a person feel strong or healthy again

Chapter 1

MATCH DAY

Volleyball players, like many other athletes, are creatures of habit. At the high levels of the sport, athletes like to have set routines, whether the match is the opening round of the AVP New Orleans Open or the finals of the FIVB Volleyball world championship. The consistency of a routine is a key part of match-day preparation.

GET SOME REST

It sounds simple enough—go to bed, and get some sleep. But high school and college students have busy schedules, as do pro players, so it might not be that simple in many cases. Giving your body the proper amount of rest often requires the same sacrifice and dedication that training does. Especially at higher levels, athletes will likely find themselves traveling a lot, and dealing with changing time zones and erratic playing schedules can be challenging.

Sleep is necessary to optimize both your physical and mental condition. Players should try to get between eight and nine hours of sleep the night before they compete. If that is not possible because of travel or other factors, several players

> *Set from a consistent body position and hand position so you can be deceptive. If you arch your back too much, the blockers will know you are setting back. And if you take the ball too far in front of you, the only place you can set is forward.*
>
> *– Lindsey Berg, U.S. Olympic silver medalist*

> "Sand is an entirely different game than indoor volleyball. Even if you are an amazing indoor player, your skills are going to take time to transition to the sand." – Lisa Rutledge, 2009 AVP Best Defensive Player

find naps to be beneficial. Players prefer naps of varying lengths, ranging anywhere from thirty minutes to four hours. Without the proper rest, athletes report feeling foggy and have trouble focusing, which obviously has a negative impact on performance. Irritability is another reported symptom. A good night's sleep, on the other hand, leaves players energized. When well rested, their minds are sharp, and they can think clearly and react quickly.

Many players also tout the **restorative** benefits of sleep. Sleep gives the body the time and ability to heal and recover, which is especially critical when playing matches on back-to-back days.

Players use many different tricks to help them get good sleep. Many recommend taking melatonin supplements, a natural chemical that is known to promote sleep. Players will also wear eye masks and earplugs to block out distractions while sleeping. Light, noise, and a warm room are enemies of good sleep.

Coaches can help ensure their players are optimizing sleep in a couple of ways. First, they should make players track their sleep in a journal, so they see where shortfalls are occurring and work to eliminate them. Also, coaches can schedule practices so that they

Sleep helps players like these AVP pros at a tournament in Arizona heal and recover from the previous day, so their bodies are ready for the new day's action.

do not take place too early or too late in the day, where possible. This is especially the case at the high school and college levels, where coaches should be aware of the student workload on their players and be sure they are allowing sufficient time for both practice and studying.

PERFORMANCE NUTRITION

The sport of volleyball requires a lot of dynamic, high-energy movements, the kind that burn a lot of energy. So on match day, players need to fuel their bodies for the intense activity to come. The primary fuel should be carbohydrates. These are compounds the body burns to create energy for the muscles, and without a healthy dose, players will fatigue quickly during play.

Matches can take place at different times of the day. According to the Performance Institute, good carbohydrate sources that are also low in fat and high in protein include the following:

"Sleep is very important for muscle recovery. I find that if I'm not sleeping well I tend to be a little more sore the next day. I drink a protein shake before I go to bed and it seems to help me sleep."

– Phil Dalhausser, 2008 Olympic gold medalist

Volleyball players need a carb-heavy meal on game day to provide the energy their muscles need to perform at a high level.

"The more colorful the food, the better. I try to add color to my diet, which means vegetables and fruits."

– Misty May-Treanor, three-time Olympic gold medalist

Breakfast: cereal, pancakes, waffles, toast, bagels, oatmeal, grits, orange juice, fruit

Lunch: low-fat sandwiches made with bread or rolls (choose turkey, ham, or roast beef), pasta with low-fat toppings or sauce, salads, fruit

Dinner: lean meat (turkey, chicken, or pork) or fish, potatoes, pasta, rice, vegetables, salad, fruit, low-fat yogurt

Snacks: pretzels, fruit, yogurt, energy bars, cereal

Eating a high-carb prematch meal will allow you to maximize your energy during the match. This meal should be eaten about four hours before the match is scheduled, if possible. A high-carb snack should then follow one to two hours prior to playing. If you are playing a morning match, do not sacrifice sleep to eat. Instead, eat a high-carb meal the night before and then have that snack in the same prematch time frame the next morning.

Besides the carbs to boost energy, the body also needs water to compensate for the fluids that will be lost from sweating during strenuous play. Dehydration can have a significant negative effect on even a well-rested, well-fed body. In the hour before play, try to drink about twenty ounces of water. During the match, hydrate whenever breaks in play allow, ideally drinking about four ounces every fifteen minutes. On average a player should drink at least sixty ounces of water during a match, including twenty ounces of water (or a low-sugar **electrolyte** drink) at halftime.

Good nutrition continues after the match as well. A post-match meal should again be high in carbohydrates with some lean protein. If playing a tournament, players should keep their bodies nourished and help their recovery by eating a high-carb snack along with a few ounces of protein within twenty minutes of playing each match. Water should be consumed as thirst dictates as well.

STRETCH IT OUT

After a good night's rest (or a nap) and the right meal, players arrive at the court and need to get their bodies ready to play. The prime factor in this goal is proper stretching. Tight muscles are likely to cause the body to perform poorly and are also much more likely to be injured. The remedy is to increase the flexibility of your muscles, which is done most effectively by stretching.

One of the key areas for volleyball players is the hips. Constant crouching in a defensive position often leads to short, tight hip flexors, which can

> *"When it comes to attacking as well as hitting a jump serve, the first step toward the point of contact where you're hitting the ball needs to be in a direct line from where you've started to where the ball is."*
>
> *– Jeff Nygaard, two-time NCAA Player of the Year*

> " You can get your sand legs by going for a run in the sand. I used to try and go three times a week for twenty minutes on top of my training. It can be a job just to get your legs ready. "
>
> — Nicole Branagh, 2008 U.S. Olympian

A coach helps a player with a prematch calf stretch. Players can use stairs to do this stretch on their own.

limit range of motion in the joint. The most effective stretch for the hip flexors is the lunge. In this stretch, using alternating legs, the player stands with feet shoulder width apart and steps far forward with one leg until the thigh is parallel to the floor. The stretch should be held on each side for about five seconds.

The quadriceps muscles in the thigh play a large part in supporting the knee, an oft-injured part of a volleyball player's anatomy. To stretch out the quads, lie on your side with your shoulder on the floor. Grab the top of the foot on the top leg, and pull your heel toward the glutes. Hold three pulls for five seconds each, and then turn over and switch legs.

The complementary muscles to the quads are the hamstrings, the muscles between the knees and the glutes, which get tremendous use in a jumping sport like volleyball. To stretch the hamstrings, sit on the floor with one leg extended and the other bent with the sole against the knee of the outstretched leg. Reach out, and try to grab the ankle, toes, or heel of the outstretched leg, going only as far as necessary to feel a good stretch in the muscle. Try holding three stretches, going a little further each time, and then repeat on the other leg.

Stretching the calves will help protect the Achilles tendon and lessen the likelihood of developing foot problems like plantar fasciitis. For a good calf stretch, find a staircase, and hold both handrails while standing on the bottom stair. Raise one leg, and stand on the edge of the stair with the ball of the other foot. Lower the heel of the foot below the level of the stair, and hold for a few seconds. Repeat five times before switching legs.

The gluteus maximus do a lot of work during play, especially during side-to-side movements. They can be stretched from a sitting position on the floor. Extend both legs, then raise the right knee and cross the right leg over the left, keeping the knee up. Grab the knee, and pull it to your chest. Hold three pulls for five seconds each, then switch legs.

The groin is another area that suffers from strain injuries. Stretch the groin muscles from a seated position on the floor. Put the soles of your feet together, and slowly press your knees toward the floor until you feel the stretch in your inner thigh.

Overhead arm movements happen frequently when playing volleyball, so stretching the posterior shoulder muscles and rotator cuff is important. Lie on your left side, and extend your left arm out in front of you. Then bend your left arm, so your fingertips are pointing toward the ceiling. With your right arm push your left arm down, keeping your palm toward the floor and your left arm in a ninety-degree angle until you feel a gentle stretch. Repeat on both sides.

WARM IT UP

Once the body has been stretched, it is time to get it warm before the match starts. Drills are an efficient way to do this while working on game skills as well. There are a number of different drills to try.

1. **Ball toss:** With a partner, throw a ball back and forth across the width of the court with your hitting arm to loosen the shoulder (duration: two minutes).

> **"** Passing is not about a big swing. It's all in bending your legs and moving your feet. **"**

– Holly McPeak, International Volleyball Hall of Fame inductee

Elena Rusu warms up with a passing drill before a match in Bucharest, Romania, in 2014.

2. **Spike drill:** With a partner, have him or her lob balls to you from across the width of the court that you can spike back in one bounce to complete a full range of motion shoulder warm-up (duration: twenty reps).

3. **Set drill:** With a partner, stand ten feet apart, and set the ball back and forth to each other to work the forearms. Do ten reps each, and repeat from twenty feet apart.

4. **Pass drill:** This is the same as the set drill using passes rather than sets.

5. **Pepper drill:** With a partner, stand ten feet apart, and have him or her toss the ball. Pass it back, so he or she can spike it, and practice digging the return. Alternate roles throughout (duration: three minutes).

6. **Defensive drill:** This is a full squad drill. The team lines up about ten feet apart facing the coach. A designated setter takes a position to the coach's right. The coach throws the ball at the first player in the line, who must find a way to pass it to the setter. That player then becomes the setter, and the original setter joins the end of the line (duration: ten minutes).

7. **Hitting drill**: This is a full squad drill. Three lines are formed consisting of outside hitters, middle hitters, and right side hitters. The coach tosses the ball to a designated setter who alternately sets balls for one of the three lines.

8. **Serving drill**: This is a full squad drill. The squad divides in half with players lining up on opposite baselines. Players all have balls and practice serves back and forth across the net.

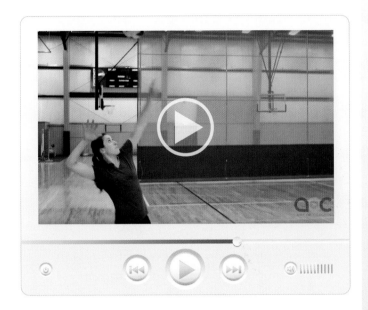

Watch NCAA Coach Terry Liskevych's tips on improving serving technique.

GET IN THE ZONE

So much of mental preparation comes down to confidence. Without it, all the physical preparation and game planning leading up to the match are in **jeopardy**. Confidence is not a trait but rather a skill that can be improved.

First of all, an athlete should look the part. Walk with confidence, so keep your head up and shoulders back. How you use your body matters. Walk, move, and even breathe like someone who expects to succeed—it all makes a difference.

Next, be sure you know your stuff. You should have studied the opposition and know your coach's game plan well. Being certain of these things will help breed the confidence that you can execute them.

American Kerri Walsh Jennings is a three-time world and Olympic champion.

Many players also believe in affirmations to help their confidence. Affirmations are positive sayings that they tell themselves. The theory is that what you say and how you say it can impact your confidence and focus. Here are examples of positive affirmations:

- I can set at a high level during the whole match.

- I am a consistent server.

- I will anticipate my opponent's next shot.

- I am hitting with power today and improving with every attempt.

- I get better as I go and will make the correct adjustments.

The key is to keep negative thoughts from entering your mind. Don't think about don'ts. "Don't shank it, don't shank it, don't shank it" is not a good example of the kind of thoughts a player wants in his or her head before attempting a serve. This is a negative thought and promotes the wrong approach. A more appropriate thought might be: "This serve is going in. It's going to be an ace. My jump serve is really on point today."

Imagery is a technique used by many players to imagine these positive thoughts as actions being executed. Many players believe it to be the most effective method of mental preparation. Imagery involves not only visualizing yourself making a positive play but also imagining what that will sound and feel like as well.

TEXT-DEPENDENT QUESTIONS:

1. Name some of the tricks players use to help them get good sleep.

2. According to the Performance Institute, what are three examples of good carbohydrate sources that are also low in fat and high in protein?

3. List four drills volleyball players use to warm up.

RESEARCH PROJECT:

Take some time, and put together a pregame routine for yourself. Be detailed in each element, outlining specific numbers of repetitions for drills, and so on. Be sure to be specific to your primary position. Outline meals, rest, and all the necessary components that you feel could help best prepare you before a big game.

WORDS TO UNDERSTAND:

adrenaline: a substance that is released in the body of a person who is feeling a strong emotion (such as excitement, fear, or anger) and that causes the heart to beat faster and gives the person more energy

overpronation: excessive rotation of the medial bones in the midtarsal region of the foot inward and downward so that in walking, the foot tends to come down on its inner margin

psychological: directed toward the will or toward the mind specifically in its conative function

Chapter 2

THINK THE GAME

IT'S ALL IN YOUR MIND

There is a saying that practice is 95 percent physical and 5 percent mental, but matches are 95 percent mental and 5 percent physical. By the time the match rolls around, hours of practice have been invested in technique and mechanics. The physical side of the game should be automatic. But even if you have perfect technique and quick reflexes, these will do you no good if you lack a positive attitude. It is important to be in a good frame of mind when playing.

How can that good frame of mind be achieved? First, your attitude must be in check. If you are not relaxed enough to concentrate fully on the game and your role on the team, you will be less effective as a player and more susceptible to injury. To control nerves and anxiety, there are many different methods, so it's best to explore all the options and find what works for you. Some people listen to loud music to pump themselves up, others prefer deep breathing and relaxation, and some find that meditation helps them to clear their minds. Other techniques include stretching and yoga, which warm you up physically and at the same time relax and prepare you mentally. Any of these methods will help lessen your anxiety about the game. They will help you focus on what is really important: your performance individually and as a team player.

> You never really feel ready. There is always something more that your mind tells you you should be doing. However, the trick is to be able to show up and perform no matter what the circumstance.
>
> – Natalie Cook,
> Australian Olympic gold medalist

The next step is to mentally rehearse in preparation for your performance. Think about your duties on the court and how you have been coached to play. Recall what you have done wrong and what steps you have taken to correct those mistakes. Think of the last time you performed well; what set that performance apart? What made the difference? That is what you need to succeed.

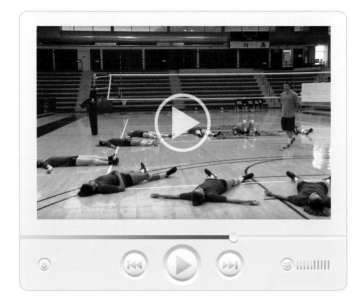

The Santa Clara University NCAA women's team incorporates visualization into its tournament preparation.

The technique known as imagery is popular with modern athletes. The more realistic your visualization, the more it will help you to mentally rehearse and feel comfortable when it comes time to perform. Imagine the roar of the crowd, the sound of sneakers on the wooden floor, and the feel of the volleyball soaring into the air as you strike it. Helping yourself relax both physically and emotionally will improve your play by making you feel more at ease on the court.

Sometimes, however, passion overpowers play, and in your urge to spike the ball through the floor, mistakes happen. It is important for each player to find the most productive level of energy in terms of performance. You must have enough **adrenaline** flowing in your blood to sharpen your eyes, ears, and reactions but not so much that you lose control. It is essential that you strike a balance between the will and the skill required to perform.

Players like American Kerri Walsh use imagery before matches to imagine themselves making great plays, like this block during a tournament in China.

That balance is different for every player, and only with practice and experience will you be able to tell where you need to be.

Too much adrenaline can have adverse effects. Your coordination will not be as good as it should be, and you will be unable to focus your attention effectively. This means that you will be more prone to injuries, including muscle tears, sprains, and strains. If you lose a few points on the spin, it is especially important that you remain cool. Concentrate on getting the basics right, try to read your opponents' plays, and take charge. Above all, don't lose your head. If your fear of failure is too great, you will be too emotional to perform. If you and your teammates panic, you have already lost.

ALWAYS LOOK FOR THE POSITIVE

Some experts will say it is best to immediately put poor performances in the past, but there is a different approach. Instead, try turning that negative experience into a positive one by looking at your performance and figuring out how you could do better next time. Ask your coach how you could improve your game, and then, with your coach's guidance, create a training strategy to address the improvements you need to make. This is not a difficult step to take, but it is the first and a very important one.

Players must always believe they are going to win. Without a positive attitude, weeks of physical preparation could be wasted.

Be sure to set goals that are realistic and trackable. If being out of shape is your problem, set a goal to improve your level of fitness within a month. Run 400 yards (365 m), and record your time. Aim to reduce that time by a realistic margin, perhaps 3 to 5 percent, after a month's training. Do not push yourself too hard as setting a goal you cannot attain will only discourage you.

Refresh your goals continually as you hit them. Your ultimate goal should be to become a complete player, equally good at serving, setting, spiking, blocking, bumping, digging, and diving. You will enjoy the results, your game will certainly improve, and you will inspire your teammates to play at a higher level, too.

PLAYING IT SAFE: EQUIPMENT AND ACCESSORIES FOR INDOOR VOLLEYBALL

Volleyball equipment is designed to both help player performance and maximize player safety. For example, good pairs of shoes and kneepads are essential for the indoor game. For beach volleyball, a hat and sunscreen should be at the top of the list.

It all starts with a good pair of shoes. The brand and model is not nearly as important as that the shoes are reasonably new and fit well.

How to Choose a Volleyball Shoe

Footwear specific to volleyball came around later than it did for other sports. Today, however, there is a good selection of shoes out there for the unique movements and stresses indoor volleyball athletes put on their shoes. The one characteristic that most defines a volleyball shoe is its gum rubber sole. This feature gives the shoe more traction on the hardwood court than a running or cross-training sneaker would. But there are several other distinct attributes that define these shoes. Volleyball shoes also provide better support for lateral movement and have special padding in the front of the shoe that acts as a shock absorber for all the jumping the sport requires. Some shoes are marketed as optimal for either defensive or attacking purposes. Most shoes are primarily constructed of either a synthetic mesh or leather. Each has its advantages. Mesh allows the foot to breathe, while leather is more durable. Which to use is the player's preference. Both are lightweight, with the leather shoe weighing about two ounces more for women and four ounces more for men. Some shoes even have ventilation and suspension systems. Advanced technology comes with a higher price point. Shop around to find the shoes that are right for you.

A good pair of shoes can last a relatively long time, but a player should always look for telltale signs of wear. Many players complaining of knee problems, for example, buy new shoes and find their problems significantly reduced. Volleyball is a sport that places great demands on footwear. Players need shoes that have a high-grip sole and that can cope with takeoffs, landings, and sudden changes of direction. All of these combine to shorten the life of a pair of volleyball shoes. Make sure that yours are up to the job.

A good pair of shoes is the most essential equipment for an indoor player.

In the sport of volleyball, ankles take a beating. If you injure your ankles often and find the injuries are getting increasingly serious and recovery is taking longer each time, you may need to use an ankle brace. You will also need to strengthen the ankle and increase its flexibility, but wearing an ankle brace will prevent the likelihood of further damage.

The brace will also make you more aware of your ankle's position in space, and you will find yourself moving in a way that is less likely to result in injury. There are **psychological** advantages as well. Rather than worrying about your ankle, you will be able to concentrate on your role in the game.

Most volleyball courts are constructed with wood floors, which are more forgiving than other hard surfaces. Despite this, diving for a ball could still easily damage a kneecap, hip, elbow, or shoulder, which could cause a great deal of pain and keep you out of the game for months. Wearing knee and elbow pads will help protect your joints against possible injuries during a fall.

Knees are right up there with ankles as the body part that gives players the most trouble. There are several classifications of braces and sleeves to help

Knee and elbow pads help protect against acute injuries.

support the knee:

- functional—gives additional support for injured knees

- rehabilitative—limits movement of the knee while it heals

- prophylactic—protects from traumatic impact

- patellofemoral—helps the kneecap (patella) move smoothly over the knee joint

Of these, the functional and rehabilitative ones have shown to be effective. Some people, however, believe that wearing braces may actually increase the likelihood of injury, either because this allows the athlete to overload a knee that is not strong enough to deal with the weight or because the brace's external support structure serves to weaken the knee's own natural support structure. Most athletes who wear them, however, believe they help, and that factor alone is important.

It is crucial that a brace or sleeve fits the player correctly. If not, it is worse than useless. Also, you need to wear it whenever you are increasing the load on your knee, which means during warm-up just as much as when training or playing a match. Remember, too, that your knee brace is the least important aspect of preventing knee injury or of rehabilitation after an injury. Stretching and strengthening the legs, and managing your fitness program correctly, are far more important.

Next in line among the areas that players tend to injure are the hands and wrists. Maneuvers such as the floater serve and the spike place great amounts of pressure on the wrist, and throughout the course of a season, strains are not uncommon. Likewise, it is not unusual for fingers and thumbs to be sprained when blocking.

Players have choices when it comes to protecting these areas, such as wearing gloves or using strapping. If a finger is sprained, you can prevent further injury when training and playing by strapping it to the next finger, a

A pair of quality sunglasses is the most important piece of equipment for beach players.

procedure known as buddy taping. There are also finger braces on the market.

BEACH VOLLEYBALL

With a soft surface like sand, the need for shoes, kneepads, and elbow pads goes away. The likelihood of ankle and knee injuries is also greatly reduced. The outdoor game, however, includes one big danger that does not factor into the indoor game—the sun.

Ultraviolet (UV) rays are always present, even when it is cloudy. For this reason, players, officials, and spectators need to wear a reliable, broad-spectrum sunscreen. Beach volleyball players spend a great deal of time in the sun, and failure to apply a protective layer of sunscreen will increase their risk of skin cancer.

A baseball-style cap will help protect your face from the sun's UV rays. It will also help keep the sun out of your eyes.

Many beach players consider a good set of sunglasses to be the most crucial piece of equipment. Without them, sunlight—whether directly, glinting off the ocean, or reflecting off something shiny—can leave you with temporary blind spots. Make sure your sunglasses are also UVA and UVB resistant. Eyes, like skin, can burn. If your eyes are exposed to sunlight for as little as six hours without protection, they will feel gritty and may begin to water profusely. These are symptoms of sun blindness, and the only cure is to keep your eyes cool and covered for eighteen hours.

The beach game does still involve hitting a ball, so as with the indoor game, players will find that their fingers, thumbs, and wrists take a battering. Strap or brace as you would for the indoor game.

Practicing and learning good technique is the best method to help prevent these issues from happening in the first place.

OTHER SAFETY GEAR

Knee problems that are persistent likely require a trip to the doctor. One thing the doctor may recommend is arch support. If your feet tend toward **overpronation** and roll inward, your kneecap will not move smoothly in its

groove. This is what causes much of the knee pain experienced by volleyball players. Arch supports correct overpronation and should ease any knee pain. If over-the-counter products do not help, consider having some custom-made.

A good pair of shoes should give you all the shock absorption you need, but players can get heel cushions that are designed to help reduce compression throughout the leg during landing. If you do find yourself landing heavily on your heels during a game, work on building up your calves and improving your balance.

Aches and pains are inevitable in a physically demanding sport like volleyball. Always warm up and cool down properly, but if you are feeling the effects of your playing or practicing, you may want to use some of the supports available in good sports stores.

Achilles tendon supports, hamstring supports, back supports, and elbow and shoulder supports are all widely available. If you think that wearing one of these will make a difference in the way you feel and play, or if your coach has recommended you buy one, you should do so. Or you could adjust your training schedule and make sure it includes a little more strengthening work in those areas. The results will be longer lasting.

TEXT-DEPENDENT QUESTIONS:

1. What are a few of the different methods volleyball players use to control nerves and anxiety on match day?

2. Volleyball is a sport that places great demands on what kind of equipment?

3. What is the biggest danger to the health of a beach volleyball player that is not an issue for indoor athletes of the sport?

RESEARCH PROJECT:

Do some research on the affects of adrenaline on the body. What is it, what produces it, and how is it either helpful or a hindrance to the body? What is the fight or flight response?

WORDS TO UNDERSTAND:

aerobics: a system of physical conditioning involving exercises (such as running, walking, swimming, or calisthenics) strenuously performed to cause a marked temporary increase in respiration and heart rate

coordination: the ability to move different parts of the body together well or easily

exerted: having put (oneself) into action or tiring effort

Chapter 3

TRAIN FOR SUCCESS

GETTING THE BODY READY

A focused mind will be of limited use if the body it controls is not ready to perform or injured. Unless you warm up or do some form of stretching exercise before practicing, sudden bursts of activity are likely to cause injury. Your muscles, ligaments, and tendons will not be flexible enough to endure strenuous physical activity.

It is a good habit to incorporate both a warm-up and a cooldown, and when combined with your mental preparation, this habit provides you with a routine that will help you focus your mind on the challenge ahead.

Stretching to ensure muscles and ligaments are flexible is an effective way to help avoid injuries.

Making the body more limber and preparing it for prolonged exertion are the goals of a warm-up. Wear an extra layer of clothing to hold in the warmth you generate, and keep this layer on until you are called onto the court for the game. The ideal warm-up routine includes three distinct aspects: stretching, **aerobics**, and practice.

Any good warm-up should always start with stretching. Attempting physical activity with tight muscles and tendons is just asking for injury. While general stretches are important, be sure to also choose specific stretches that work on the muscle systems you are about to use the most. For volleyball, this means the shoulders, back, groin, legs, knees, and ankles.

Stretch steadily and gradually, holding each stretch for at least thirty seconds. Do not bounce or pump the stretch position as this could snap a tendon or ligament. Slowly extend the stretch up to, but not beyond, the point where you feel it begin to pull. Work on complementary areas. For instance, stretch your quadriceps for thirty seconds, and then stretch your hamstrings for thirty seconds. Stretch only as far as you comfortably can, and pay specific attention to areas that have recently recovered from injury.

> *When I show up to the beach, it's just about getting my body ready. I jog, do dynamic stretches, and then I connect with my partner right away. Doing the warm-up together, talking about how you're feeling about the team you're going to play, I think that's all really important dialogue.*
>
> *–Kerri Walsh Jennings, four-time U.S. Olympian*

Once you are loose, it is time to get the body warm. Aerobic exercise is designed to raise the heart and respiration rates slowly. As you begin to breathe more quickly and deeply, your lungs take in more air. This, combined with your increasing heart rate, raises the level of oxygen in the blood. This helps your body convert stored energy and increases the flow of blood throughout the body. The increased heart rate also raises body temperature, warming and loosening the muscles and tendons.

It will not take much time to get a light sweat going. About ten minutes of brisk walking or jogging will do the job, and it will also help you clear your mind and focus on the task ahead. After this, try a few short on-the-spot sprints.

Now your body is ready to practice or train safely and effectively. Practice should be a run-through of all the different maneuvers your body will be performing in a competitive match, beginning with the most gentle.

For example, start with something basic like triangle passing, an exercise to raise your perception and **coordination**. It will also stretch and warm your shoulders and limber up your hips, knees, and ankles. Stand in a triangle with two other teammates, and pass the ball between you. Do this for three to five minutes.

By this stage, you should be prepared for specific drills, both physically and mentally. If there is any part of your body that is not ready for what lies ahead, you will find out about it during this warm-up. If so, consult your coach about whether you should continue.

Watch NCAA champion Andor Gyulai demonstrate proper hitting technique.

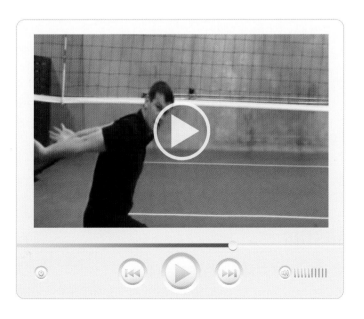

An Italian player practices the spike drill before a match against Cuba.

PRACTICE DRILLS

SERVING

Serving Underhand

- Stand facing the opposition court with the left foot forward.

- Hold the ball at waist height with the left hand, and draw back the right arm. Simultaneously lean forward, placing your weight on your left foot, and swing the right arm toward the ball.

- Withdraw the left hand just before contact, hit the ball with the palm or heel of the right, then follow through with the right arm.

Serving Overhand

- Stand facing the opposition court with your left foot forward and the ball at chest level in your left hand. Raise and draw back your right arm.

- With your wrist stiff and your arm straight, toss the ball vertically eighteen to twenty-four inches (forty-five to sixty centimeters).

- Simultaneously lean forward, placing your weight on your left foot, then swing the right arm forward to hit the ball with the heel of the right hand, and follow through.

PASSING

READY PASSING POSITION

When preparing to receive the ball, stand with your feet spread, your knees bent, with your hips over your ankles, your shoulders ahead of your knees, and your arms straight and at ninety degrees to the torso.

PASSING

Forearm pass, when receiving a serve, or dig (the same maneuver but defensively), when receiving an attack:

- Position yourself to meet the ball straight on, using shuffle steps (sideways steps) to cover ground.

- As the ball approaches, draw the hands together, and move the arms from the shoulder, keeping them straight.

- Contact the ball at hip level, just above the wrists and with hands together, then follow through.

- If you want to change the direction of your return, make sure the follow-through is in the direction the ball should go.

Practice passing with your teammates by standing in a circle and passing to each other. Give yourselves enough space to move to the ball.

DEFENSE

READY DEFENDING POSITION

- Stand with your feet spread, knees bent, hips back, and shoulders forward, with your hands ahead of you, palms facing up.

- Try to remain still while digging the ball, and aim to dig the ball in an arc of twenty feet (seven meters) above the court, passing through the plane of the net cord about three feet (one meter) to your side of the net.

BLOCKING

Keep your feet planted, ready to jump, and shoulders square to the net.

The Polish men's national team prepares for a serving drill during warm-ups at the 2016 Olympics in Rio de Janeiro.

- Keep your hands a ball's width apart, thumbs vertical, fingers diagonal, and arms straight.

- When timing your jump, watch the setter to find out where the ball is heading.

Once the hitter has been identified, watch him or her approach and see where the eyes are looking to indicate the direction of the hit. Then move to block it.

OFFENSE

SETTING
This sets up the ball for spiking and is also used as an overhand pass.
- Face the target with your left foot forward and your weight on the right foot, knees bent and feet spread.

- Raise your hands six to eight inches (fifteen to twenty centimeters) ahead of your forehead as if cupping the ball, looking through the triangle made by your first fingers and thumbs, and keeping hands, forehead, and hips in a line.

- Just before you contact the ball, straighten your arms and legs while keeping your eye on the ball, then follow through in the direction you want the ball to go.

- For setting, your goal is to drop the ball just inside the sideline, three feet (one meter) to your side of the center line.

HITTING
This maneuver is used for attacking and spiking.
- If using a three- or four-step run-up, make sure your last step is the longest and most powerful. Plant your left foot, then swing both arms ahead of you, and take off vertically with both feet slightly apart.

- Extend your left arm out ahead of you, and draw the right arm back, above, and behind your shoulder with your right arm bent.

- Drop the shoulder, and then, keeping the right arm slightly bent, use the heel or palm of the right hand to make contact with the ball immediately above and ahead of the forehead.

SIDEBAR

Train Like a Pro

Volleyball requires a high level of fitness to compete at a high level. This is especially true in the beach game as the surface is demanding and there are only two players on a team. Unlike the indoor version, players are involved in every point. In 2016, *Sports Illustrated* magazine named beach volleyball star Kerri Walsh Jennings one of the ten fittest female athletes on the planet. At thirty-eight, the triple gold medal-winning mother of three is still in world-class shape. Not to be outdone, her current partner April Ross is no slouch herself. The thirty-four-year-old Ross, a two-time NCAA national champion indoors at the University of South California, has a Herculean workout schedule. Here's what Ross says about what it takes each week to compete as an Olympian in beach volleyball:

- Practice on the beach: two and a half hours per day, six mornings per week—"Our coach specifically runs a really high-cardio practice, so you're dead tired afterwards."

- Weight training: two and a half hours per day, four afternoons per week—"I used to subscribe to the higher reps, lower weight type of workout, but now I've been doing less reps with higher weights, and I really like that for explosiveness."

- Beach circuit workout: two to three days a week

  - Lateral shuffle with medicine ball: ten reps per round
  - Burpees: five reps per round
  - Triangle sprints: two circuits per round
  - Sled pull sprint: two sprints per round
  - Mountain climbers: fifteen reps per round
  - Suicide sprints: two circuits per round
  - Star drill with medicine ball: two circuits per round

TRAINING

Effective training should always be specific to your sport of focus. For example, while certain hockey drills may be great to get you into shape and make you a better athlete, they won't do you very much good as a volleyball player. In volleyball, it is important to focus on your shoulders, hips, knees, and ankles as these are the joints that receive the most wear and tear from performance. Also, learning how to improve your reaction time, muscle control, stability, and extension will lessen your chance of injury. It is important to focus on a number of types of training, including weight training, plyometrics, and cardio.

Doing squats strengthens the muscles of the thighs, hips, and buttocks.

STRENGTH TRAINING

Lower body exercises:

- **Squats:** Begin in a standing position, slowly bending the knees and hips until you are in a sitting position; hold for ten to fifteen seconds, stand up straight, and repeat. This exercise strengthens the muscles of the thighs, hips, and buttocks.

- **Leg press:** Using a leg press under your coach or trainer's supervision, you can strengthen your entire lower body. Sitting below the sled, push it upward with your feet, and slowly lower back down until your knees are bent halfway, then extend again.

- **Deadlift:** Pull the barbell from the floor with both hands until your body is fully extended. Begin pushing from the heels, and bring your hips forward, being careful not to pull with your lower back. This exercise strengthens the lower back but can also cause serious injury, so be sure to work with a trainer to learn proper technique.

- **Bench step-ups:** Using just your body weight or holding lightweight dumbbells in each hand, stand in an upright position. Stand directly in front of a step bench that is eighteen to twenty-four inches (forty-six to sixty-one centimeters) high. Place one foot (your lead foot) flat on the bench. With most of your weight on the heel of the lead foot, forcefully push off with the lead leg and assume a standing position with both feet on the bench. Repeat this exercise using the other leg as the lead leg.

UPPER BODY EXERCISES

- **Pullover:** This exercise will help strengthen most muscles in the upper body through a full range of motion, especially the shoulders, which are prone to injury. Pullovers improve the overhead motion used consistently by volleyball players. Hold the dumbbell close to your body and lie down carefully on your back on a bench. Bend your knees in a comfortable position, and hold the dumbbell vertically, with the farther end resting in your palms and your arms straight out above your head. Lift your arms so they are right above your face, keeping your elbows straight, then slowly lower the arms back down. Perform two to four sets of ten to fifteen repetitions.

- **Push press:** Grasp a barbell from the floor with an overhand grip, slightly wider than shoulder width. Position the bar chest high with your torso tight, and pull your head back. Dip your body by bending the knees, hips, and ankles slightly. Explosively drive upward with the legs, driving the barbell up off the shoulders and extending your arms overhead. This exercise strengthens your shoulders and prevents future injury.

- **Explosive push-ups:**
  Start by getting into the push-up position, and lower yourself on the ground. Then, explosively push up so that your hands leave the ground. Catch your fall with your hands and immediately lower yourself into a push-up again and repeat, without allowing your chest, stomach, or thighs to touch the ground.

Explosive push-ups help improve upper-body strength for more power in the hitting game.

PLYOMETRIC TRAINING

These exercises cause muscles to exert maximum force in short time intervals, which increases power:

- **Depth jumps:** Stand on a box with your toes close to the edge. Step (do not jump) off the box and land on both feet. Immediately jump up and reach with both hands toward the ceiling, keeping your momentum from stepping down. Keep your time on the ground to a minimum, jumping right away once you touch the ground.

- **Over-the-back toss:** Stand with your feet slightly wider than hip width apart. Have a partner or trainer stand about ten yards (nine meters) behind you. Grasp a medicine ball, and lower the body into a semi-squat position. Explode upward, extending the entire body, and throw the ball behind you as far as you can, generating power in your legs. Catch the ball on a bounce from your partner, and repeat.

- **Lateral high hop:** Stand to the left of a box, and place your right foot on top of it. Push off the box using the right leg only, and explode vertically as high as possible. Drive the arms forward and up for maximum height. Land with the opposite foot on the box, and repeat, alternating back and forth.

- **Squat throw from chest:** Stand with your feet slightly wider than hip width apart and your knees slightly bent. Hold a medicine ball at chest level, and squat down to a parallel position. Quickly explode up, and jump as high as you can. As you start your jump, throw the ball as high as possible. Retrieve the ball, and repeat the exercise.

CARDIOVASCULAR TRAINING

Volleyball is not an endurance sport. Instead of working on increasing endurance, volleyball players should be better at exerting quick, short bursts of power, which is known as anaerobic exercise. But a player must also be able to perform in a game without tiring.

- **Line drills:** Commonly known as suicide drills, this exercise helps increase your endurance but also focuses on short bursts of speed and energy. Beginning at the far end of a gym or sports field, your coach will set up evenly spaced distances along the length of the floor.

Plyometric exercises like box jumps help develop explosive power

Starting at the end, run to the first distance, and immediately run back to your starting point. Without resting, turn around and run back in the opposite direction, but this time, run even further to the second distance, then return to the starting position. Continue this drill until you have run all the way to the other end of the floor and returned to the beginning, stopping at each distance along the way.

COOLDOWN

Following training or practice, put on an extra layer of clothing, so you do not cool down too fast, which would mean that your soft muscle tissue would become sore and stiff. Slow down your body by jogging gently for five minutes, then finish off with ten minutes of stretching, paying particular attention to the areas you have **exerted** most.

TEXT-DEPENDENT QUESTIONS:

1. Give three examples of practice drills.

2. What are the joints that receive the most wear and tear from performance during the sport of volleyball?

3. Name two plyometric training exercises.

RESEARCH PROJECT:

Look into what is required to put together an effective off-season training program. What types of non-volleyball activities are best to keep players in shape? How might off-season training vary by position?

 WORDS TO UNDERSTAND:

compression: the act, process, or result of squeezing into less space to provide pressure

supination: a corresponding movement of the foot and leg in which the foot rolls outward with an elevated arch

tendinitis: inflammation of a tendon

Chapter 4

TAKING CARE OF THE BODY: INJURIES AND NUTRITION

Compared to other sports, injuries in volleyball are relatively infrequent. At the Olympic level, a volleyball player will suffer an injury after an average of twenty-five hours on the court and, at a national amateur level, after fifty hours. At this level, about half of all players can expect one injury during a season, although most injuries will be minor enough to allow resumed play within a week.

Landing or falling on the hard indoor surface is a common cause of acute volleyball injuries.

Landing from a jump is responsible for most of the injuries seen in volleyball. Players have to jump when both attacking and defending. Most hand injuries in volleyball are caused by blocking. The spike is the second-most hazardous activity, placing the ankle at risk, and jumping places great demands on the knee. The more volleyball you play, the more likely it is that you will suffer from the single most common overuse injury: jumper's knee.

Volleyball injuries fall into two main categories: acute and overuse. An acute injury tends to be traumatic, caused by a single event such as a sprain, whereas overuse injuries become more of a problem as you spend more time on the court. Both these types of injuries are most likely to occur to the ankles, knees, hands, and wrists, with the ankle being particularly vulnerable.

OVERUSE INJURIES

KNEES

If you have experienced a dull, aching pain usually located at the bottom of the kneecap, you have probably had jumper's knee. Technically known as patellar **tendinitis**, it is responsible for 80 percent of overuse injuries in volleyball. The more often you jump, and the more powerfully you jump, the more likely you are to suffer from it. Studies have shown that you are most likely to suffer if you are a jumper training hard to improve, if you bend your legs more than ninety degrees when jumping, and if you have been playing competitively for three to five years.

SHOULDERS

Overuse injuries to the shoulder are also common in swimmers and tennis players. Spiking and serving are chiefly responsible for shoulder tendinitis—particularly the floater serve, where the follow-through is held back, thus limiting the spin given to the ball. Symptoms include generalized pain in the shoulder area and a feeling of weakness.

Learning arm deceleration is very important because most shoulder injuries occur after the ball s spiked.

– Marcin Jadoga, AVP pro

LOWER BACK

Constant serving and spiking can result in a dull ache at the base of the spine. Much of the power for jump serving and spiking is generated in the lower back, and overexertion can lead to problems. Landing also jars the lower back. Over time, these two factors may combine to cause pain.

TREATMENT

Here is how an acute injury typically manifests itself:

- First, there is damage to the tissue—muscles or ligaments—that causes bleeding. In the more severe cases, this bleeding can be seen on the surface as bruising.

- Second, the body protects the damaged area by swelling and inflaming the area. This protects from further impacts and prevents any movement that could increase the damage.

- Third, the body begins to repair the damage that has been done. Two to three days after the injury occurs, new blood vessels begin to form around the damaged area. Three to five days later, new tissue—a scar—is formed.

Scar tissue needs higher maintenance to remain supple. If it is not stretched and exercised regularly, especially during the healing process, scar tissue will shrink. This leaves the damaged area greatly reduced in flexibility and prone to stiffness.

P.R.I.C.E.

This is a treatment method that takes the standard R.I.C.E. method one step further by adding the element of protection.

Protection

Take immediate action to get off the court as quickly as possible as soon as you feel an injury or any unexplained pain. Move to a place or position where you can take pressure off the injury.

Rest

Try to rest the injured area completely for up to twenty-four hours.

Ice

Icing the area reduces inflammation, dulls the pain, and limits the damage to the soft tissue. This should occur as soon as possible. Crushed ice should be placed in a plastic bag, then wrapped in a towel, and wrapped around the injury. Applying ice directly can burn the skin. You can also use a bag of frozen peas wrapped in a towel. Apply ice for no longer than fifteen minutes. If the treatment is becoming painful, stop using ice therapy, and use cold therapy instead.

Stiintas Stoyanova puts an ice pack on her leg after she suffered an injury during the Romanian Women's Volleyball Cup. Ice is used to prevent swelling immediately after an acute injury.

49

Place small towels in a bucket of iced water, wring one out, and wrap it around the injury. Replace with a cold towel when the first towel warms up. You can also place hands or feet in the bucket, but check on them often. Repeat ice or cold therapy every three hours. It is particularly effective after you have been exercising.

Compression
Applying pressure to the injury will limit internal bleeding and swelling. Apply a **compression** bandage as soon as possible after the injury but only after you have completed your first session of ice therapy. Make sure that the bandage provides pressure both above and below the injury area and is tight enough to be effective but not so tight that it keeps blood from circulating.

Elevation
Immediately raise the injured area higher than your heart. This is done to limit bruising and swelling. Elevation should be employed as often as possible and can be combined with ice therapy or compression.

INJURY PREVENTION
There is much you can do to protect yourself from acute injuries. Think about the injuries you have had and how they happened. Then plan your training schedule to address the areas in which you are weak.

Rest is the only way to avoid overuse injuries. You may not have to stay off the court completely, though. Studies have shown that jumpers suffer the most overuse injuries, so the recommended course of action is simple: jump less! Working hard on jumping training makes little difference to the height you can reach or the power you develop. Good jumpers are good jumpers whether they train or not. If you train hard most days and feel your knees, shoulders, and lower back aching, you might consider changing games for a time and play beach volleyball instead. You will still be enhancing your skills, but statistically, you will be five times less likely to suffer injuries because sand is much more forgiving than a hard court.

NUTRITION
Training and nutrition go hand in hand in enhancing athletic performance. It is often said that you cannot out-train a bad diet. Athletes must be

careful to eat a proper blend of nutrients to make sure their bodies and minds perform as well as they possibly can. This does not just mean eating healthy foods but also choosing when to eat, how much to eat, and whether to take dietary supplements. Of course, when you choose a new diet or supplement, you should consult with a nutritionist, doctor, or some other expert. It is best not to make up your own nutrition program.

CHOOSING A DIET

What you eat is crucial to an athlete. Volleyball is a cardio-intensive sport with running, diving, and jumping. This is especially true for athletes playing the beach variety of the sport. Typically, a player has to eat considerably more than other people do in order to maintain higher energy levels. The United States Food and Drug Administration (FDA) suggests that the average American should eat about 2,000 calories a day; for a male high school- or college-level athlete, a 3,000- to 4,000-calorie diet is more common. There are three main food groups to consider when choosing a diet: carbohydrates, protein, and fats.

CARBOHYDRATES

Carbohydrates are foods rich in a chemical called starch, which is what the body breaks down to get energy. Starchy foods include breads and grains, vegetables such as potatoes, cereal, pasta, and rice. There is no one-size-fits-all formula that can exactly dictate what an athlete's carb consumption should be. A general rule is that in season or during times of intense training, athletes should eat about five grams of carbs for every pound of body weight. In the off-season or during periods of lower training levels, it should be about two to three grams per pound. The body uses carbs strictly for fuel, so if they are not being burned, they are turned into fat and stored. Therefore it is important to adjust carb intake based on activity level. Athletes should not eat heavily processed carbohydrates such as white sugar and white flour. These simple carbs are quickly broken down into sugars, which the body processes into fats if it does not immediately burn them off. The best carbohydrate choices for an athlete are complex types like pasta and whole-grain foods as well as starchy vegetables. A nutritious diet avoids empty calories or those provided by food that lacks other nourishment, like processed sugar and starches.

Beach volleyball pro Angie Akers discusses her nutrition plan.

ANGIE AKERS
on diet & nutrition
WWW.PROTIPS4U.COM

PROTEIN

Unlike carbohydrates, protein is used within the body. Proteins are important chemicals used to perform specific functions inside the body's cells. Our bodies can break down proteins that are found in foods and use them to build new proteins that make up our muscles and bones. During periods of intense training and activity, the body needs more protein to repair damage to muscles. Not eating enough protein can cause an athlete to lose muscle mass and negatively affect the ability to perform. The Academy of Nutrition and Dietetics recommends athletes consume about one-half to three-quarters of a gram of protein for every pound of body weight. During the season or heavy training, that number should be closer to a full gram per pound. This higher ratio is also true if an athlete is trying to build muscle mass. The best sources of proteins are lean meats and dairy products (such as milk or cheese) as well as eggs and certain types of soy, beans, and nuts.

FATS

Lots of times, we think of fats as bad for us because eating too much of them is unhealthy. However, fat is an important ingredient needed to make

White breads and sugar contain empty calories and no significant nutrients. Athletes should avoid these foods.

our bodies work correctly. They help to balance hormone production, support cell growth and protect your organs, among other functions. Without fats, our bodies cannot absorb certain vitamins as well as they should. Also, our skin and hair need some amount of fat to grow correctly. However, fats should still be eaten in moderation as they are higher in calories than protein or carbs. No more than seventy grams a day is recommended. All fats are not created equal, however. Trans fats and saturated fats found in processed foods are high in bad cholesterol, which clogs arteries and is bad for the heart. The best sources of fat are vegetable oils, olive oil, and nuts.

DIETARY SUPPLEMENTS

Ideally, a balanced diet would provide our bodies with all the nutrients it needs. However, for many varying factors, eating optimally is not always possible. Dietary supplements are available to fill dietary gaps created by a deficient diet.

In discussing dietary supplements, this does not include banned performance-enhancing substances. Instead, the focus here is on supplements that contain vitamins, minerals, and other compounds that help the body absorb nutrients or recover more efficiently. When properly used, supplements can improve overall health and performance, but you should always consult a doctor or other expert before using them to augment your diet or training program. Some examples of common supplements include vitamin tablets and protein shakes or powder.

VITAMIN TABLETS

For many reasons, we do not always get the vitamins and nutrients we need. Often, this is because our diets are not as balanced as they should be. Sometimes, it is because the foods that are available to us have been processed in such a way that they lose nutrients. If you know or suspect that a certain key vitamin is underrepresented in what you are eating, in many cases, the necessary vitamins can be obtained from vitamin supplements. These supplements, which are usually taken as a pill, can either contain a balanced mixture of vitamins and nutrients (multivitamins) or contain a single vitamin or mineral that our diet is lacking. The best way to avoid this issue is to work hard to eat right whenever possible.

Multivitamins can fill the gaps in athletes' nutrition when there are times they cannot eat a balanced diet.

Protein shakes can help provide efficient protein boosts when needed, such as immediately following matches or workouts.

PROTEIN SUPPLEMENTS

Getting enough protein from the food you eat can be difficult as well. For athletes, eating protein immediately after a workout is recommended (in order to refuel your body), but most people either don't feel up to or do not have the time to spend cooking or preparing themselves a meal immediately after a workout. That is where protein shakes come in handy. These are protein supplements sold in powder form that look and taste like milkshakes when blended with water but contain no dairy products. Protein shakes deliver a high ratio of protein to carbohydrates and calories. They are not meant to replace meals. Many other necessary nutrients are gained from a balanced diet that cannot be replaced by protein shakes, regardless of how fortified they may be.

STAYING HYDRATED

The body needs water more than it needs any other nutrient. If you are not getting enough water, your performance will suffer in spite of any preparation or balanced diet. Dehydration occurs when your body doesn't have enough water. Symptoms include fatigue, dizziness, and headaches. No athlete can perform at his or her best if not properly hydrated. Proper hydration should be maintained not only at matches but throughout training as well. The body does not store water, so we need to constantly maintain its supply. The American College of Sports Medicine recommends these guidelines for athletes:

Before Exercise: 16-20 ounces within the two-hour period prior to exercise
During Exercise: 4-8 ounces every fifteen to twenty minutes during exercise
Post Exercise: 24 ounces for every one pound of body weight lost during exercise

Have a full bottle at the bench to make sure you can drink during time-outs and between sets to keep you performing your best on the court.

Players should be careful to stay fully hydrated when training or playing.

TEXT-DEPENDENT QUESTIONS:

1. How are ankle sprains measured?

2. What does P.R.I.C.E. stand for?

3. When does dehydration occur?

RESEARCH PROJECT:

Start a nutrition journal. For one month, track your daily intake of key nutrients, including carbohydrates, fat, protein, and water. Based on your weight and training routine, map out a plan for what you should be eating on which days, and assess how well you did sticking to the plan after one month. What were the challenges to sticking to the plan?

WORDS TO UNDERSTAND:

boycotted: having engaged in a concerted refusal to have dealings with (as a person, store, or organization), usually to express disapproval or to force acceptance of certain conditions

sanctioned: explicitly or officially approved, permitted, or ratified

volleying: prolonging the back-and-forth flight of an object on its course before striking the ground

Chapter 5

VOLLEYBALL: FROM BADMINTON TO THE BEACH AND BEYOND

WILLIAM MORGAN TO THE OLYMPICS

Like its net and ball cousin basketball, the game of volleyball was invented in America at a YMCA. In 1895, William Morgan was the physical education director at the YMCA in Holyoke, Massachusetts, just ten miles from Springfield, where James Naismith had come up with basketball just four years earlier.

Morgan's original version of volleyball was called mintonette, and he intended it to be a combination of basketball, tennis, handball, and even baseball. The name was taken from the sport of badminton, where the goal is also to keep an object aloft back and forth over a central net. The first volleyball net was actually a tennis net suspended on stakes that were just six feet, six inches (two meters) high. The first ball was the inside bladder taken from a basketball. Morgan's intention was to create a game that was less physically demanding than basketball for the businessmen in his physical education classes.

Besides Karch Kiraly, there are two other names honored as the best so far in the history of the sport: male cowinner Lorenzo Bernardi and female winner Regla Torres.

Lorenzo Bernardi was a multitalented, dominant outside hitter on Italy's national indoor team for fifteen years. The six-foot, six-inch (two-meter) Bernardi first played for his nation in 1987, eventually leading his country to back-to-back world championships in 1990 and 1994, when he was named tournament MVP. Bernardi retired from playing pro club leagues in Italy in 2007 and began a coaching career in 2009. He was inducted to the International Volleyball Hall of Fame in Holyoke in 2011.

Regla Torres was inducted to the hall in 2001 after a stellar indoor career. The Cuban middle blocker played her first match with the Cuban national team at just sixteen years old in 1991. From there, she led her country to back-to-back world championships in 1994 and 1998 and three straight gold medals at the Summer Olympics from 1992 to 2000. Torres was named MVP and Best Blocker at both world championship tournaments. Outside of Torres and her Cuban indoor teammates, no other player has amassed three indoor volleyball Olympic gold medals. Only Kiraly, Misty May-Treanor, and Kerri Walsh Jennings have as many as three volleyball Olympic gold medals when beach volleyball is included.

Morgan changed the name of his game after a spectator at a demonstration suggested that because there was a lot of **volleying** (a familiar tennis term) back and forth of the ball, volleyball would be a more fitting name. Aside from the six-foot, six-inch (two-meter) high net, the game Morgan demonstrated had the following rules:

- The court was twenty-five by fifty feet (eight by fifteen meters), so it could easily be played indoors at various YMCAs.

- It would have two teams of any number of players so that it could accommodate differing-sized groups.

- Each match consisted of nine innings.

- Each team could serve three times per inning (three outs).

- There was no limit to the number of times each team could contact a ball before volleying it back to the other team.

- Each server was allowed two tries to get the ball over the net.

- A point would be awarded to the other team if the ball hit the net (except in the case of a faulty first serve), if the ball failed to be served back to the other side before hitting the ground, or if the ball was hit outside of the court by the team that had just returned it over the net.

Morgan submitted his game for review at the 1896 YMCA Physical Director's Conference, and the first official game was played in July of that year. Four years later, a ball was designed specifically for the sport, and in the next twenty years, the game spread across the country and beyond to Canada, Cuba, South America, and the Philippines.

The first FIVB World Championship was held in 1949 with just ten entries. The modern event features the best twenty-four of 140 registered countries from around the world.

The rules evolved over time as well. The United States Volley Ball Association (now USA Volleyball) was formed in 1928, and the Fédération Internationale de Volleyball (FIVB) was formed in France in 1947.

Today, the game is the second-most popular team sport in the world, behind only soccer in terms of participation.

The first world championships in the sport was held in 1949 in Czechoslovakia, with a women's version added in 1952. The event is now held every four years. Volleyball was added as an Olympic medal sport in 1964.

Beach volleyball is first believed to have been played in Hawaii in 1915, becoming popular on the beaches of Santa Monica, California, in the 1920s. Played with teams of two rather than six a side, it was officially recognized by the FIVB in 1987 and added as an Olympic event in 1996.

THE SOVIETS, KARCH KIRALY, AND KERRI WALSH JENNINGS

The volleyball teams from the Soviet Union dominated the early Olympic years. Women's teams won four of the first seven gold medals, and Soviet men won three of the first five and won medals in the other two. In the first five Olympics to include volleyball as a medal sport, there was a Soviet team on the podium for every men's and women's tournament. In total the Soviet men and women combined for six golds, three silvers, and a bronze from 1964 to 1980.

In 1980, Charles "Karch" Kiraly was entering his junior year at the University of California-Los Angeles, in which he would lead UCLA to a second volleyball national title in three years. The following year, Kiraly led the Bruins to a third title in his four-year tenure and was named All-American for the fourth time. He also made the U.S. national team that year and looked forward to facing the dominant Soviets at the 1984

Now the head coach of the U.S. women's indoor team, Californian Karch Kiraly was named Greatest Volleyball Player of the Twentieth Century by FIVB.

Olympics in his hometown of Los Angeles. The Soviets **boycotted** those Olympics, however, and Kiraly led the U.S. team to an easy gold medal win over Brazil.

In 1986, Kiraly led the American men to the world championship title for the first and only time, beating the mighty Soviets in the semifinals. But the true test would come at the Seoul Olympics in 1988, when the two volleyball titans met in the gold medal match. Kiraly and the Americans dropped the first set to the Soviets but then stormed back to win the last three 15–10, 15–4, and 15–8 (the set-winning total was changed to 25 in 1999 when side-out scoring was eliminated) and the gold. Kiraly was named the Olympic tournament MVP.

> "Practice like it's competition and compete like it's another day on the practice court.
>
> – Karch Kiraly, three-time Olympic gold medalist

Kiraly retired from indoor volleyball after playing professionally in Italy through 1992. That is when he began his long and prestigious career as a beach volleyball star. Over twenty-five seasons, he won 148 tournaments, the most in the sport's history. When beach volleyball became an Olympic medal sports at the Atlanta Games in 1996, Kiraly and partner Kent Steffes won the inaugural gold medal. In 2001, the FIVB named Kiraly co-Greatest Volleyball Player of the Century. He retired from playing in 2007. He took over as head coach of the women's national indoor team in 2012 and led them to a bronze medal in 2016 in Rio.

The women's national indoor team has never won a gold medal, something Kiraly hopes to change. On the beach, however, American women have been dominant, led by career wins and medals leader Kerri Walsh Jennings.

Like Kiraly, Walsh Jennings grew up in California and was a standout indoor player. She was named a four-time All-American at Stanford, at the time only the second player so honored. Walsh Jennings led the Cardinal to two national titles and was National Player of the Year as a senior in 1999. In 2000, she made the indoor team that represented the United States at the Sydney Olympics. After that, she switched to the sand.

As a beach player, Walsh Jennings became the most decorated woman in volleyball history. She has more than 130 career wins, most of those with longtime partner Misty May-Treanor. Walsh Jennings and May-Treanor are also three-time Olympic champions as well, winning back-to-back-to-back gold medals in 2004, 2008, and 2012. After May-Treanor retired in 2012, Walsh Jennings teamed with April Ross for the 2016 Olympics, where the pair won bronze.

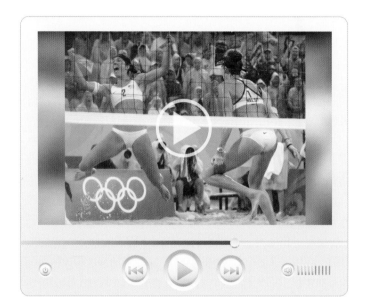

Check out this profile of American stars Kerri Walsh Jennings and Misty May-Treanor.

THE BEACH AND THE FUTURE OF VOLLEYBALL

Indoor volleyball is an immensely popular sport, especially outside of the United States. Twenty-nine countries have professional indoor volleyball leagues for both men and women. In terms of athlete participation, only soccer is higher, again, outside the United States. In America, indoor volleyball participation is actually declining. Statista.com counted indoor volleyball participants in the United States as dropping from 8.19 million players in 2008 to just over 6 million in 2013, for about a 25 percent decrease.

The sport has tried to revamp itself and adjust to a marketplace that is

Three-time Olympic beach volleyball gold medalists Kerri Walsh Jennings (L) and Misty May-Treanor of the United States.

Two-time U.S. Olympic medalist April Ross digs a shot in a 2013 match against Kazakhstan.

increasingly fractured and distracted. The FIVB made a fundamental rule change in 1999, going from side-out to rally scoring. In side-out scoring, only the team serving could score points. If the other team won the rally, no point was awarded, rather the serve changed teams instead. Under this system, matches took much longer to play, even though sets were won at just 15 points. Under rally scoring, a point is given on every rally, regardless of which team serves. It takes 25 points to win a set with rally scoring, but still matches take about thirty minutes less on average, which FIVB officials want as that makes the sport more marketable for television. That was nearly two decades ago, however, and at least in the United States, the sport is not growing as hoped.

In America, the future growth of the sport may come from outside. Thanks in no small part to the star power of players like Walsh Jennings and Kiraly, beach volleyball has continued to grow in popularity over the decades, both in the United States and abroad. In the United States, beach volleyball participation grew from 3.32 million to 5.14 million between 2006 and 2012. At the college level, the NCAA **sanctioned** its very first collegiate national championship in the sport in 2016. The University of Southern California beat Florida State University in the finals. The NCAA first sanctioned beach volleyball in 2012 at select schools. By 2016, the sport earned a national championship tournament as it now has more than forty schools in Division I. Interestingly, the NCAA only offers the sport to women. Title IX regulations mean only a certain number of men's sports can be offered without adding to the women's side, and due to the large number of scholarships offered for men's football, adding beach volleyball for men is tricky for the NCAA.

Internationally, beach volleyball is growing as well. Participation increases have been reported in England, continental Europe, Australia, New Zealand, and elsewhere. International stars have found their place in the sport's lore as well. Indoor stalwarts like Brazil's three-time world champion and Olympic gold medalist Giba and two-time Chinese Olympic medalist Feng Kun inspired beach star compatriots Emanuel Rego (also three-time world champion and Olympic gold medalist) and world champion and FIVB Most Outstanding Player Zhang Xi.

Beach volleyball has thrived in places like Brazil, China, and even Germany. The FIVB Beach Volleyball World Tour has operated since 1989. The Brazilians, specifically ten-time champion Emanuel Rego and eight-time winners Larissa França and Juliana Silva, have dominated the tour. It makes stops in places like Ft. Lauderdale, Florida, Norway, Germany, Croatia, and Canada but also countries with no beaches like Austria and Switzerland. In fact, countries around the world are building beach courts miles inland

Three-time world champion and Olympic gold medalist Emanuel Rego of Brazil.

from the nearest shore as the game becomes more popular.

In the United States, that popularity is reflected in the television coverage of beach volleyball. In the 2008 coverage from Beijing, broadcaster NBC aired more coverage of beach volleyball than any other sport. Four years later from London, the broadcast of the women's semifinal matches (American teams won both) was the most watched in the United States since a 1976 women's gymnastics broadcast. In 2016, beach volleyball was again one of the anchor sports in prime time, airing live along with tape-delayed swimming, track, or gymnastics coverage. Does all of this mean that beach volleyball is the future of the sport? In the cases mentioned, a large part of NBC's decision to cover beach volleyball live as they did was certainly tied to the fact that Walsh Jennings and May-Treanor were immensely popular and on the way to winning medals. They were true stars and well-publicized faces of the U.S. team in general. As for the sport itself, it has certainly come a long way and is undeniably poised to at least challenge its indoor cousin for most popular version. In terms of what audiences want to watch in America, beach volleyball is already winning. Time will tell if the rest of the world will follow that trend.

Anouk Vergé-Dépré played at the Rio Olympics for Switzerland, a country that has medaled at the Olympics despite having no beaches.

Larissa França, 2011 world champion, competes in Brazil at a match during the 2016 Rio Olympics.

TEXT-DEPENDENT QUESTIONS:

1. What was William Morgan's original version of volleyball called?

2. In what year was volleyball added as an Olympic medal sport?

3. In what year did the NCAA sanction its very first collegiate national championship in beach volleyball?

RESEARCH PROJECT:

Which is the greatest volleyball-playing country in the world? Based on major international results, star players, and other metrics (be sure to outline your criteria), rank the top five countries, and provide the rationale for your ranking. Do the countries change if you consider beach volleyball as well?

SERIES GLOSSARY OF KEY TERMS

Acute Injury: Usually the result of a specific impact or traumatic event that occurs in one specific area of the body, such as a muscle, bone, or joint.

Calories: units of heat used to indicate the amount of energy that foods will produce in the human body.

Carbohydrates: substances found in certain foods (such as bread, rice, and potatoes) that provide the body with heat and energy and are made of carbon, hydrogen, and oxygen.

Cardiovascular: of or relating to the heart and blood vessels.

Concussion: a stunning, damaging, or shattering effect from a hard blow—especially a jarring injury of the brain resulting in a disturbance of cerebral function.

Confidence: faith in oneself and one's abilities without any suggestion of conceit or arrogance.

Cooldown: easy exercise, done after more intense activity, to allow the body to gradually transition to a resting or near-resting state.
Dietary Supplements: products taken orally that contain one or more ingredient (such as vitamins or amino acids) that are intended to supplement one's diet and are not considered food.

Dynamic: having active strength of body or mind.

Electrolytes: substances (such as sodium or calcium) that are ions in the body regulating the flow of nutrients into and waste products out of cells.

Flexible: applies to something that can be readily bent, twisted, or folded without any sign of injury.

Hamstrings: any of three muscles at the back of the thigh that function to flex and rotate the leg and extend the thigh.

Hydration: to supply with ample fluid or moisture.

Imagery: mental images, the products of imagination.

Mind-Set: a mental attitude or inclination.

Overuse Injury: an injury that is most likely to occur to the ankles, knees, hands, and wrists, due to the excessive use of these body parts during exercise and athletics.

Plyometrics: also known as "jump training" or "plyos," exercises in which muscles exert maximum force in short intervals of time, with the goal of increasing power (speed and strength).

Positive Mental Attitude (PMA): the philosophy that having an optimistic disposition in every situation in one's life attracts positive changes and increases achievement.

Protein: a nutrient found in food (as in meat, milk, eggs, and beans) that is made up of many amino acids joined together, is a necessary part of the diet, and is essential for normal cell structure and function.

Quadriceps: the greater extensor muscle of the front of the thigh that is divided into four parts.

Recovery: the act or process of becoming healthy after an illness or injury.

Resistance: relating to exercise, involving pushing against a source of resistance (such as a weight) to increase strength. Strength training, or resistance exercises, are those that build muscle. They create stronger and larger muscles by producing more and tougher muscle fibers to cope with the increasing weight demands.

Strategy: a careful plan or method.

Stretching: to extend one's body or limbs from a cramped, stooping, or relaxed position.

Tactics: actions or methods that are planned and used to achieve a particular goal.

Tendon: a tough piece of tissue in the body that connects a muscle to a bone.

Training: the process by which an athlete prepares for competition by exercising, practicing, and so on.

Warm-Up: exercise or practice especially before a game or contest—broadly, to get ready.

Workout: a practice or exercise to test or improve one's fitness for athletic competition, ability, or performance.

FURTHER READING:

Schmidt, Becky. *Volleyball: Steps to Success (Steps to Success Activity Series).* Champaign, IL: Human Kinetics, 2015

Cain, Brian. *The Mental Game of Volleyball: Competing One Point At A Time (Masters of the Mental Game).* North Charleston, SC: CreateSpace Independent Publishing, 2015

Correa, Joseph. *The Ultimate Guide to Volleyball Nutrition: Maximize Your Potential.* North Charleston, SC: CreateSpace Independent Publishing, 2014

Dr. Dunphy, Marv. *Volleyball Essentials.* North Charleston, SC: CreateSpace Independent Publishing, 2014

INTERNET RESOURCES:

NCAA Volleyball: *http://www.ncaa.com/sports/volleyball-women/d1*

Volleyball Nutrition Guide: *http://www.sportsrd.org/wp-content/uploads/2015/01/Volleyball_Sports_Nutrition_WEB.pdf*

American Academy of Orthopaedic Surgeons: *http://orthoinfo.aaos.org/topic.cfm?topic=A00183*

College Volleyball Scholarships: *http://www.athleticscholarships.net/volleyballscholarships.htm*

VIDEO CREDITS:

Watch NCAA Coach Terry Liskevych's tips on improving serving technique: *http://x-qr.net/1F0c*

The Santa Clara University NCAA women's team incorporates visualization into its tournament preparation: *http://x-qr.net/1DJw*

Watch NCAA champion Andor Gyulai demonstrate proper hitting technique: *http://x-qr.net/1DTs*

Beach volleyball pro Angie Akers discusses her nutrition plan: *http://x-qr.net/1Cqr*

Check out this profile of American stars Kerri Walsh Jennings and Misty May-Treanor: *http://x-qr.net/1Ftq*

PICTURE CREDITS

QR CODES AND LINKS TO THIRD-PARTY CONTENT

INDEX

In this index, page numbers in ***bold italics*** font indicate photos or videos.

ABOUT THE AUTHOR

Peter Douglas is a former journalist, reporting on both sports and general news for many years at television stations in various locations across the US affiliated with NBC, CBS and Fox. Prior to his journalism career he worked with the Boston Red Sox Major League baseball team. An avid writer and sports enthusiast, he has authored 16 additional books on sports topics. In his downtime Peter enjoys family time with his wife and two young children and attending hockey and baseball games in his home city.